The art of boxing. By Daniel Mendoza, P.P.

Daniel Mendoza

The art of boxing. By Daniel Mendoza, P.P.
Mendoza, Daniel
ESTCID: T132832
Reproduction from British Library
With a half-title.
Dublin : printed by M. O'Leary, 1792.
xi,[1],36p.,plate ; 12°

Eighteenth Century
Collections Online
Print Editions

Gale ECCO Print Editions

Relive history with *Eighteenth Century Collections Online*, now available in print for the independent historian and collector. This series includes the most significant English-language and foreign-language works printed in Great Britain during the eighteenth century, and is organized in seven different subject areas including literature and language; medicine, science, and technology; and religion and philosophy. The collection also includes thousands of important works from the Americas.

The eighteenth century has been called "The Age of Enlightenment." It was a period of rapid advance in print culture and publishing, in world exploration, and in the rapid growth of science and technology – all of which had a profound impact on the political and cultural landscape. At the end of the century the American Revolution, French Revolution and Industrial Revolution, perhaps three of the most significant events in modern history, set in motion developments that eventually dominated world political, economic, and social life.

In a groundbreaking effort, Gale initiated a revolution of its own: digitization of epic proportions to preserve these invaluable works in the largest online archive of its kind. Contributions from major world libraries constitute over 175,000 original printed works. Scanned images of the actual pages, rather than transcriptions, recreate the works *as they first appeared.*

Now for the first time, these high-quality digital scans of original works are available via print-on-demand, making them readily accessible to libraries, students, independent scholars, and readers of all ages.

For our initial release we have created seven robust collections to form one the world's most comprehensive catalogs of 18th century works.

Initial Gale ECCO Print Editions collections include:

> ***History and Geography***
> Rich in titles on English life and social history, this collection spans the world as it was known to eighteenth-century historians and explorers. Titles include a wealth of travel accounts and diaries, histories of nations from throughout the world, and maps and charts of a world that was still being discovered. Students of the War of American Independence will find fascinating accounts from the British side of conflict.

Social Science
Delve into what it was like to live during the eighteenth century by reading the first-hand accounts of everyday people, including city dwellers and farmers, businessmen and bankers, artisans and merchants, artists and their patrons, politicians and their constituents. Original texts make the American, French, and Industrial revolutions vividly contemporary.

Medicine, Science and Technology
Medical theory and practice of the 1700s developed rapidly, as is evidenced by the extensive collection, which includes descriptions of diseases, their conditions, and treatments. Books on science and technology, agriculture, military technology, natural philosophy, even cookbooks, are all contained here.

Literature and Language
Western literary study flows out of eighteenth-century works by Alexander Pope, Daniel Defoe, Henry Fielding, Frances Burney, Denis Diderot, Johann Gottfried Herder, Johann Wolfgang von Goethe, and others. Experience the birth of the modern novel, or compare the development of language using dictionaries and grammar discourses.

Religion and Philosophy
The Age of Enlightenment profoundly enriched religious and philosophical understanding and continues to influence present-day thinking. Works collected here include masterpieces by David Hume, Immanuel Kant, and Jean-Jacques Rousseau, as well as religious sermons and moral debates on the issues of the day, such as the slave trade. The Age of Reason saw conflict between Protestantism and Catholicism transformed into one between faith and logic -- a debate that continues in the twenty-first century.

Law and Reference
This collection reveals the history of English common law and Empire law in a vastly changing world of British expansion. Dominating the legal field is the *Commentaries of the Law of England* by Sir William Blackstone, which first appeared in 1765. Reference works such as almanacs and catalogues continue to educate us by revealing the day-to-day workings of society.

Fine Arts
The eighteenth-century fascination with Greek and Roman antiquity followed the systematic excavation of the ruins at Pompeii and Herculaneum in southern Italy; and after 1750 a neoclassical style dominated all artistic fields. The titles here trace developments in mostly English-language works on painting, sculpture, architecture, music, theater, and other disciplines. Instructional works on musical instruments, catalogs of art objects, comic operas, and more are also included.

The BiblioLife Network

This project was made possible in part by the BiblioLife Network (BLN), a project aimed at addressing some of the huge challenges facing book preservationists around the world. The BLN includes libraries, library networks, archives, subject matter experts, online communities and library service providers. We believe every book ever published should be available as a high-quality print reproduction; printed on-demand anywhere in the world. This insures the ongoing accessibility of the content and helps generate sustainable revenue for the libraries and organizations that work to preserve these important materials.

The following book is in the "public domain" and represents an authentic reproduction of the text as printed by the original publisher. While we have attempted to accurately maintain the integrity of the original work, there are sometimes problems with the original work or the micro-film from which the books were digitized. This can result in minor errors in reproduction. Possible imperfections include missing and blurred pages, poor pictures, markings and other reproduction issues beyond our control. Because this work is culturally important, we have made it available as part of our commitment to protecting, preserving, and promoting the world's literature.

GUIDE TO FOLD-OUTS MAPS and OVERSIZED IMAGES

The book you are reading was digitized from microfilm captured over the past thirty to forty years. Years after the creation of the original microfilm, the book was converted to digital files and made available in an online database.

In an online database, page images do not need to conform to the size restrictions found in a printed book. When converting these images back into a printed bound book, the page sizes are standardized in ways that maintain the detail of the original. For large images, such as fold-out maps, the original page image is split into two or more pages

Guidelines used to determine how to split the page image follows:

- Some images are split vertically; large images require vertical and horizontal splits.
- For horizontal splits, the content is split left to right.
- For vertical splits, the content is split from top to bottom.
- For both vertical and horizontal splits, the image is processed from top left to bottom right.

THE ART OF BOXING.

BY

DANIEL MENDOZA, P. P.

DUBLIN:

Printed by M O'LEARY, 113, Capel-street.

1792.

PREFACE.

AFTER the many marks of encouragement bestowed on me by a generous public, I thought that I could not better evince my gratitude for such favours, than by disseminating

to

to as wide an extent, and at as cheap a rate as poffible, the knowledge of an ART; which though not perhaps the moft elegant, is certainly the moft ufeful fpecies of defence. To render it not totally devoid of elegance has, however, been my prefent aim, and the ideas of coarfenefs and vulgarity which are naturally attached to the Science of Pugilifm, will, I truft, in a great meafure, be done

done away, by a candid perufal of the following pages. *Boxing* is a national mode of combat, and is as peculiar to the inhabitants of this country as *Fencing* to the French; but the acquifition of the latter as an art, and the practice of it as an exercife, have generally been preferred, in confequence of the objection which I have juft ftated as being applicable to the former. That objection,

I hope,

I hope, the present **Treatise** will obviate, and I flatter myself that I have deprived Boxing of any appearance of brutality to the learner, and reduced it into so regular a system, as to render it equal to fencing, in point of neatness, activity, and grace.

The Science of Pugilism may, therefore, with great propriety,

priety, be acquired, even tho' the scholar should feel actuated by no desire of engaging in a contest, or defending himself from an insult.

Those who are unwilling to risque any derangement of features in a real boxing match, may, at least, venture to practise the Art from sportiveness; and sparring is productive of health and spirits, as it is

both

both an exercife and an amufement.

The great object of my prefent Publication has been to explain with perfpicuity, the Science of Pugilifm, and it has been my endeavour to offer no precepts which will not be brought to bear in practice, and it will give me peculiar fatisfaction and pleafure sure to understand, that I have attained my *first* object, by having taught any man an easy regular System of so useful an Art as that of Boxing.

D. MENDOZA.

BOXING.

THE first principle to be established in Boxing is, to be perfectly master of the equillibrium of the body, so as to be able to change from a right to left-handed position; to advance or retreat striking or parrying; and to throw the body either forward

forward or backward without difficulty or embarraffment.

The fecond principle to be eftablifhed is, the pofition of the body, which fhould be in an inclining pofture, or diagonal line, fo as to place the pit of the ftomach out of your adverfary's reach; the upper part of your arm muft ftop or parry the round blow at the head; the fore-arm, the blows at the face and ftomach; and the elbows, thofe at the ribs; both knees muft be bent, the left leg advanced, and the arms directly before your throat or chin.

It

It must be an invariable rule to stop or parry your adversary's right with your left, and his left with your right; and both in striking and parrying, always to keep your stomach guarded, by barring it with your right or left fore-arm.

It is always better to avoid a blow by throwing the head and body back, at the same time covering the pit of the stomach, than to attempt to parry it.

Both hands must never be up or down at the same time. If your adversary strikes either at your face, stomach, or side,

with

with his left hand, parry or ſtop with your right, covering the ſtomach with your left; if he ſtrikes with his right, let your left oppoſe it, covering your ſtomach with your right.

It is proper to exerciſe the ſcholar in changing both arms and legs from alternate poſitions of right-handed to left-handed, and to make him maſter of the equillibrium of the body, advancing and retreating.

LESSON

LESSON I.

Master strikes with his left arm at your face.

Parry with your right fore-arm, barring at the same time your stomach with your left fore-arm, throwing the head and body back.

Master strikes with his right at your face.

Parry with your left fore-arm, barring at the same time your stomach with your right fore-arm, throwing head and body back.

Master strikes round at your right ear with his left.

Parry with your right arm, turning

turning up the elbow so as to cover the side of the head, barring the stomach with the left fore-arm, and throwing head and body back.

Master strikes round at your left ear with his right.

Parry with your left arm, turning up the elbow so as to cover the side of the head, barring the stomach with the right fore-arm, throwing head and body back.

Master strikes at your stomach with his left.

Bar your stomach with your right fore-arm, keeping your left opposite his nose, throwing your head and body back.

He strikes at your stomach with his right.

Bar your stomach with your left fore-arm, keeping the right fist opposite his nose, throwing head and body back.

His left strikes at your right side.

Stop with your right elbow, keeping your left fist opposite his nose, throwing head and body back.

His right strikes at your left side.

Stop with your left elbow, keeping your right fist opposite his nose, throwing head and body back.

LESSON

LESSON II.

1, 2.

Mafter makes the feint 1, 2, at your face, ftriking firft with his left at your face, (which is the feint) in order to hit you in the face with his right.

Parry firft with your right fore-arm, and fecondly with your left fore-arm, covering the ftomach with the right fore-arm, and throwing head and body back.

Mafter feints in the fame manner, beginning with his right.

Parry firft with your left fore-arm, and fecondly with your right fore-arm, covering the ftomach ſtomach with the left fore-arm, and throwing head and body back.

His left feints at your ſtomach, to hit your face with his right.

Bar your ſtomach with your right fore-arm, and parry the blow at your face with your left fore-arm, throwing head and body back.

His right does the ſame.

Bar your ſtomach with your left fore-arm, and parry the blow at your face with your right fore-arm, throwing head and body back.

His left feints at your right side to hit your face with his right.

Stop with your right elbow, and parry his blow at your face with your left fore-arm, throwing head and body back.

His right does the same.

Stop with your left elbow, and parry with your right forearm, throwing head and body back.

N. B. Observe, that the three foregoing feints are at the face, *i. e.* 1, 2, at the face---secondly, 1 at the stomach, 2 at the face; and next 1 at the side, 2 at the face.

The

The feints at the stomach and side are not 3 as those at the face, but only 2---for example:

Master strikes 1 at the face, 2 at the stomach, with alternate arms.

Parry the *first* with the proper fore-arm, and the *second* with the proper bar; that is, if he strikes with his left at your face, and his right at your stomach, parry his left with your right fore-arm, and his right with your left across your stomach; if he strikes first with his right at your face, and his left at your stomach, parry his right with your left fore-arm, and

and his left with your right across your stomach.

Master strikes 1 at the side, and 2 at the stomach.

Parry with the proper arms, first by catching the blow on the proper elbow, and secondly, parrying the blow at the stomach the proper fore-arm; that is, if he strikes with his left first, catch it with your right elbow, and bar his right with your left across your stomach, and *vice versa* of his right.

He strikes at the face 1, and 2 at the side.

Parry each with their proper fore-arm and elbow.

He strikes at the stomach 1, and 2 at the side.

Bar the first with the proper fore-arm, and catch the other with the proper elbow.

This 2d Lesson consists of 1, 2, at the face, stomach and sides.

1 at the face 2 at the face
1 at the stomach 2 at the face } 1, 2, at the face
1 at the side 2 at the face
1 at the face 2 at the stomach } 1, 2, at the stomach
1 at the side 2 at the stomach
1 at the face 2 at the side } 1, 2, at the side
1 at the stomach 2 at the side

C LESSON

LESSON III.

1, 2, 3.

Master strikes with his left at your face 1; with his right, do. 2; with his left at your stomach 3, the blow intended.

Parry the first with your right fore-arm---the second with your left fore-arm---the third with your right fore-arm, barring your stomach, throwing the head and body backward.

Master strikes with his right at your face 1; with his left, do. 2; with his right at your stomach 3.

Parry the first with your left fore-

fore-arm---the second with your right fore-arm---the third with your left arm, barring your stomach, throwing head and body backward.

N. B. The above is one, two, three, at the stomach.

1, 2, 3,

AT THE FACE.

Master strikes at your head 1 with his left; do. 2 with his right; at your face, and 3 with his left, the intended blow.

Parry the first with your right ---the second with your left--- third with your right, your fore-arm

arm covering ultimately your ſtomach, throwing head and body back.

Maſter ſtrikes at your head 1 with his right; do. 2 his left at your face; and 3 with his right, the intended blow.

Parry the firſt with your left; ſecond with your right; third with your left, your fore-arm covering ultimately your ſtomach, and throwing head and body back.

N. B. The above is one, two, three, at the face.

1, 2, 3,

1, 2, 3,

AT THE SIDE.

Master strikes with his left hand at your head 1; his right do. 2; and his left at your side 3, the intended blow.

Parry the first with your right fore-arm---second left fore-arm---third right elbow.

Master strikes with his right at your head 1; left do. 2; right at your side, the intended blow.

Parry the first with your left fore-arm; second right fore-arm; third left elbow.

LESSON

LESSON IV.

RIPOSTS,

Master's left strikes at your face.

Parry with your right forearm, and return at his face with your left, which he catches in his open hand.

His right strikes at your face.

Parry with your left forearm, and return at his face with your right do.

Master's left strikes at your stomach.

Stop by barring with your right fore-arm, and return at his

his face with your left, which he catches.

His right strikes at your stomach.

Stop by barring with your left fore-arm, and return at his face with your right.

Master's left strikes at your right side.

Stop by catching the blow on your right elbow, and return at his face with your left.

His right strikes at your left side.

Stop by catching the blow on your left elbow, and return at his face with your right.

Master's left chops at your face.

Parry with your right forearm, and return at his face with your left.

His right does the same.

Parry with your left forearm, and return at his face with your right.

Master's left strikes at your stomach.

Parry it down with your right, and return a back-handed blow with the same hand, covering your stomach with your left arm.

Master's right strikes at your stomach.

Parry it down with your left, and return a back-handed blow with the same hand, covering the stomach with the right arm.

Master's left strikes again at your stomach.

Parry it down with your right, and return a straight blow at his face with the same hand.

His right does the same.

Parry it down with your left, and return a straight blow at his face with the same hand.

LESSON

LESSON V.

1, 2,

AT THE FACE.

RIPOSTS.

The Scholar ſtrikes 1, 2, beginning with the left.

Maſter parries with his left, and ripoſts with his left at your face.

Parry this ripoſt by catching his wriſt with your left fiſt, and ſtriking a back-handed blow acroſs his face with your left hand.

Do

Do the same with the right hand, i. e. beginning 1, 2, with your right.

This he will parry with his right, and ripoſt with the ſame, when you catch it with your right fiſt, and return a back-handed blow acroſs his face.

RIPOSTS.

1, 2, 3, at the face, beginning with the left.

Maſter will parry with his right, and ripoſt at your ſtomach with his left.

Stop this with your right fore-arm, and return with your left at his face.

1 at the face, and 2 at the stomach, beginning with your left.

This he will stop with his left, and ripost one, two, at your face, beginning with his left. Parry with your left, and return one, two, at his face.

1 at the face, 2 at the face, and 3 in the stomach, beginning with your left, keeping your right fist opposite his face.

This he will stop with his right, and ripost the same again, one, two, three, at your stomach, which you must bar.

Do the same with the other hand, i. e. beginning with your right.

This he will stop with his left, and ripost the same again, one,

one, two, three, at your ſtomach, which you muſt bar.

The ſcholar ſtrikes with his left at the face, the maſter parries, with his right, and ripoſts with his left at the ſtomach.

Knock the blow down, and return ſtrait at the face.

Do the ſame with the other hand.

D - LESSON

LESSON VI.

Scholar strikes 1, 2, at the face, beginning with the left.

Master parries, and riposts the same.

Scholar strikes 1, 2, 3, at the face, beginning with the left.

Master parries, and riposts the same.

Scholar strikes 1, 2, at the face, and 3 at the stomach, beginning with the left.

Master parries, and riposts the same.

Scholar strikes 1, 2, at the face, and 3 at the side, ditto. ditto.

Master parries, and riposts the same.

The

The <u>scholar</u> should always use himself to cover either the stomach by barring, or the head by projecting the fist.

At this period the scholar should parry and stop, but not return all feints for some time, and when perfect herein, he may

SET-TO, OR SPAR LO<u>O</u>SE.

RULES OF BOXING.

AFTER having thus explained the order of the lessons, and the proper method of practising them, I would impress on the reader's mind the following precepts, which will be brought to bear in fighting, and found equally easy and necessary.

Parry

Parry the blows of your adversary's right hand with your left, and those of his left hand with your right.

This rule ought never to be disregarded, except when you see a safe opportunity of catching a blow of his right hand if aimed at the face on *your* right, and striking him in the loins with your left; or of stopping his left-arm stroke on *your* left, and directing your right fist to his kidneys.

If your adversary aims all round blows,

Which is generally the case with a man ignorant of Boxing, you should strike straight forward,

ward, as a direct line reaches its object sooner than one that is circular.

If he gives way, or is staggered by a severe blow,

You should not be anxious to recover your guard and stand on the defensive, as this will be only giving him time to recollect himself, but take advantage of his momentary confusion, and follow up the blow.

Advancing,

Is practised by placing the right foot forward, at the same distance from your left, as your

Parry the blows of your adverſary's right hand with your left, and thoſe of his left hand with your right.

This rule ought never to be diſregarded, except when you ſee a ſafe opportunity of catching a blow of his right hand if aimed at the face on *your* right, and ſtriking him in the loins with your left; or of ſtopping his left-arm ſtroke on *your* left, and directing your right fiſt to his kidneys.

If your adverſary aims all round blows,

Which is generally the caſe with a man ignorant of Boxing, you ſhould ſtrike ſtraight forward,

ward, as a direct line reaches its object sooner, than one that is circular.

If he gives way, or is staggered by a severe blow,

You should not be anxious to recover your guard and stand on the defensive, as this will be only giving him time to recollect himself, but take advantage of his momentary confusion, and follow up the blow.

Advancing,

Is practised by placing the right foot forward, at the same distance from your left, as your

left

left is from the right in the first attitude; you then throw your left foot forward so as to resume your original position, and thus keep gaining on your antagonist as he recedes.

Retreating,

Which is used when your adversary approaches too violently upon you, or when you feel yourself embarrassed and wish to recover your guard, is practised by placing the left leg about as far behind the right, as the right in the original position is removed behind the left, then throwing the right hindmost so as to regain your former attitude, and thus continue receding from your antagonist just as the circumstances of the battle shall render necessary.

If you are long armed,

You will have an advantage over your antagonist, as your guard will keep him at a distance, and as your blows, by reaching further, will be struck with more force.

If short-armed,

Your superiory over your antagonist will consist in close fighting. You must endeavour to get within

within the compaſs of his arms, and aim ſhort ſtrait blows which will reach him before he can ſtrike at you, and if he does ſtrike at you, his fiſts will go over your ſhoulder.

If your adverſary is ignorant of Boxing,

He will generally ſtrike round blows, or plunge head-forward. If he ſtrikes round blows in an awkward ſlovenly manner, content yourſelf with aiming at his face and ſtomach, in a ſtrait forward direction. If he ſtrikes them quickly, ſtand chiefly on the defenſive----ſtopping his blows, and throwing in the return whenever you find it convenient---

venient---and when you perceive him winded, hit as faſt as poſſible, and follow up your blows. If he buts, or plunges at you headlong, you may either ſtrike ſtraight forward and catch his face on your fiſt; or turn round on your left heel, and let him fly over your thigh; or jump on one ſide, and ſtrike him with one hand as he advances, and with the other as he paſſes by.

In the preceding leſſons and precepts, I have endeavoured to explain the *Art of Boxing* perſpicuouſly, and to reduce it within

within as narrow a compass as possible. In order still further to illustrate my instructions, I have inserted a Plate in the Book—representing the guard, or first position.

If any instructions in the preceding pages appear difficult or obscure, I shall be happy to give every necessary explanation to those who will have the goodness to apply to me, for that purpose, at No. 7, Molesworth-street, Dublin, or at the Printer's hereof.

FINIS.

CPSIA information can be obtained at www.ICGtesting.com
Printed in the USA
BVOW060828160812

297925BV00003B/67/P